CITIES OF THE WORLD

# MOSCOW

BY DEBORAH KENT

**CHILDREN'S PRESS®**
A Division of Grolier Publishing
New York London Hong Kong Sydney
Danbury, Connecticut

## CONSULTANTS

**Professor Ilya Kutik, Ph.D.**
Department of Slavic Languages and Literature
Northwestern University
Evanston, Illinois

**Linda Cornwell**
Coordinator of School Quality and Professional Improvement
Indiana State Teachers Association

**Project Editor:** Downing Publishing Services
**Design Director:** Karen Kohn & Associates, Ltd.
**Photo Researcher:** Jan Izzo
**Pronunciations:** Courtesy of Laura Shear, M.A., Ph.D. candidate, Russian Language and Literature, University of Chicago, and Tony Breed, M.A., Linguistics, University of Chicago

---

NOTES ON RUSSIAN PRONUNCIATION
Most of the pronunciations in this book are exactly as they look, with the following notes: *ah* is like *a* in father; *uh* is as in hut; *o* is always long, as in vote; *oo* is as in food; *igh* is as in high; *ts* is always as in gets; *y* is always a consonant, as in you; *zh* is like the *s* in pleasure. Some sounds in Russian do not occur in English: *uy* is a vowel that sounds something like the *ih* sound in bit; *kh* is between *k* and *h*, like the *ch* in the Scottish word loch or in the composer's name Bach. If you try to say *k*, but relax and slur the sound, it will sound like *kh*.

---

Visit Children's Press on the Internet at: http://publishing.grolier.com

---

**Library of Congress Cataloging-in-Publication Data**
Kent, Deborah
    Moscow / by Deborah Kent.
        p. cm. — (Cities of the world)
    Includes bibliographical references and index.
    Summary: Describes the history, culture, daily life, food, people, sports, and points of interest in the capital of Russia and one of the largest cities in the world.
    ISBN 0-516-21193-5
    1. Moscow (Russia)—Juvenile literature. [1. Moscow (Russia] I. Title.
II. Series: Cities of the world (New York, N.Y.)
DK601.2.K45   2000                                   99-33909
947'.31—dc21                                CIP
                                                     AC

**GROLIER**
PUBLISHING

# TABLE OF CONTENTS

Gates, Domes, and Towers   page 5

Moscow Day by Day   page 9

The City on the River   page 19

From Circuses to Symphonies   page 33

Seeing the Sights   page 45

Famous Landmarks   page 56

Fast Facts   page 58

Map of Moscow   page 60

Glossary   page 61

Photo Credits   page 62

Index   page 63

To Find Out More   page 64

About the Author   page 64

Every hour on the hour, somber chimes ring out from a clock tower in Moscow. Radio and television broadcasts carry the sound of these famous chimes all over Russia. The chimes ring forth from the Savior Tower, one of twenty towers in Moscow's Kremlin. Once, the Kremlin was the home of the *tsars*, or emperors, of Russia, and of the tsars' family and courtiers. It is a vast complex of churches and cathedrals, courtyards, palaces, and ancient battlements. Seen from a distance, the Kremlin looks like a gleaming forest of domes and spires.

*Moscow* (MAHS-KOH)
*tsar* (TSAHR)
*Kremlin* (KREM-LINN)

Four magnificent gates lead into the Kremlin. A smaller rear entrance, the postern gate, opens to a once-secret passageway. This passage leads to the nearby Moskva River, and was designed as an escape route in case the Kremlin was under attack.

The word "Kremlin" comes from the Russian *kreml*, meaning "fortress." During the Middle Ages, kremlins were erected for defense in many Russian towns. But the Kremlin in Moscow took on special importance. As the centuries passed, it grew from a small walled fort to become the splendid complex that stands today. With the Kremlin at its heart, the city of Moscow spread farther and farther into the surrounding countryside.

Moscow is the capital of Russia, the largest country in the world in area. The city is a teeming center of trade and culture. Its universities and research institutes lure students from all over the globe. In Moscow, political leaders make decisions that resound across Russia and echo throughout the world.

The Kremlin is the hub of this mighty city. Like the spokes of a wheel, Moscow's streets radiate from the Kremlin in all directions.

Moscow sets the pace for the Russian people. The chimes from the Kremlin's Savior Tower proclaim the hour to the city and to the nation.

*A young Muscovite wearing a captain's cap*

*The Kremlin*

*Moskva* (MAHSK-VAH)
*kreml* (KRYEH-MULL)

I n an open-air market in central Moscow, weekend crowds walk among tables of goods. They gaze at cameras, VCRs, and color television sets. During the Communist era, such merchandise was almost unknown in Moscow. Today, it is available, but prices are high. Muscovites look with longing, yet few can afford to buy.

# MUSCOVITES AT HOME

With more than 8 million people, Moscow is the largest city in Russia. The government admits that it does not have completely accurate population figures for the city. Russian citizens need a government permit in order to live in Moscow. Thousands of people move there illegally, without permits, and are not counted in the census.

Many ethnic groups are represented in Moscow. Russians comprise the largest single group in the city. The ethnic Russians are people with roots in the present-day republic of Russia. Traditionally, most Russians belonged to the Eastern Orthodox Church. Many elaborate Orthodox churches and cathedrals stand in Moscow. Religious practices of all kinds were harshly discouraged under Communism, and more than half of the city's churches were destroyed. Since 1991, however, Muscovites have started attending church services once more.

Other Muscovites trace their origins to Belorussia, Armenia, Georgia, Ukraine, and the other republics of the former USSR. There are Tartars from central Asia, as well as Muslims, Gypsies, and Jews. Unlike most American cities, Moscow does not have ethnic neighborhoods. People of diverse backgrounds live side by side throughout the city.

Moscow is the hub of Russia's trade, finance, and industry. People flock to the city to find jobs, to attend school, and to enjoy the thrill of living in one of the world's great cities. Because so many people want to live there, Moscow has long had a serious housing shortage. During the 1950s, the government built blocks of low concrete apartment buildings.

*A girl doing her homework in a Moscow apartment*

*Opposite left: An Asian Muscovite in a suit and bow tie*

*Opposite right: A family in the living room of their Moscow apartment*

*Muscovite* (MUSK-OH-VITE)
*Belorussia* (BELL-OH-RUSH-UH)
*Armenia* (ARR-MEE-NEE-YUH)
*Georgia* (JOHR-JUH)
*Ukraine* (YOU-CRANE)

High-rise apartment houses of twenty stories and more rose in the 1960s and 1970s. Most Moscow apartments are tiny, often having only one or two rooms. But many buildings have pleasant courtyards with flowers, trees, and benches. These areas serve as the "backyard" for everyone in the building.

## *Welcome To GUM!*

GUM is one of the landmarks of central Moscow. The initials stand for Russian words meaning State Universal Store. Completed in 1893, GUM has stucco arches, walkways with wrought-iron railings, and a spectacular glass roof. Today, GUM overflows with jeans, clock radios, video games, and other offerings from the United States and western Europe. It is especially famous for its ice cream.

# GOING SHOPPING

Some high-rises have small supermarkets on the ground floor. For the most part, however, Moscow stores are widely scattered. Purchasing food, soap, and other essentials can take all day as you travel from store to store.

During the Communist era, most Muscovites had jobs, but their wages were low. After 1991, inflation soared. To make a bad situation worse, many workers were laid off. Others were forced to hold two or even three part-time jobs, just to meet family expenses. The average Muscovite earns only about $100 a month. With these wages, few can afford the high-priced goods at GUM and other stores. Instead, many shoppers turn to the "black market." Black marketeers sell goods illegally, avoiding import duties and other taxes.

Few Muscovites could afford to own an automobile under Communism. Most people traveled by bus or subway. Public transportation is still cheap and available throughout the city. But in the 1990s, more and more cars appeared on Moscow streets. For the first time, Muscovites had to cope with traffic jams.

*Right: A woman selling vegetables and spices in a small outdoor Moscow market*
*Below: A crowded Moscow bus*

„МЫ ПРИДЁМ К ПОБЕДЕ КОММУНИСТИЧЕСКОГО ТРУДА!"
В.И. ЛЕНИН

КОЛЛЕКТИВ КОММУНИСТИЧЕСКОГО ТРУДА

When Moscow was a Communist capital, the faces of Lenin and other political leaders seemed to gaze from every wall. By the end of the twentieth century, these familiar figures had disappeared. In their place were the images of film stars, models, and sports heroes. Such images were outlawed under Communism. Today, Muscovites can see most of the magazines, television shows, and movies that are popular in the United States.

Some Muscovites are thrilled by the changes in their city. They are overjoyed by the new openness, by the freedom to read, do, and say what they wish. Others are dismayed by the rampant commercialism, and by the host of problems that seem to follow in its wake. For the first time, Moscow is plagued by homelessness, illegal drugs, youth gangs, and street crime.

*This red silk banner honoring laborers displays the familiar face of Lenin, which was common during the Soviet era.*

Some people lament the passing of Communism. They had less freedom in the old days, but life was safer and simpler. "I work much harder than I did in the old days, and sometimes that makes it hard to remember what we've gained," says a Moscow teacher who sells used clothes on the weekends. "Freedom is sweet, but it's also a heavy, heavy load."

## Moscow Underground

Moscow's subway system, known as the Metro, is one of the grand achievements of the Communist era. Metro stations are like art museums, adorned with mosaics, statues, paintings, and chandeliers. Each day some 6 million passengers speed to their destinations along 250 miles (402 kilometers) of tunnels beneath Moscow's streets.

*This homeless Armenian girl begs for money near Red Square.*

# FAIR WEATHER AND FOUL

Snow begins to fall on Moscow in the middle of October. By November, the ground has a thick blanket of snow that usually lasts until April. The Moskva River freezes solid, but work crews carve a wide channel to let boats pass. Giant icicles, some weighing 100 pounds (45 kilograms) or more, festoon tall buildings.

*Above: A young Muscovite bundled up against the cold*

*Right: A Russian man relaxing in Gorky Park*

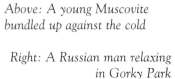

Falling icicles can be a real hazard. A special team of workers climb the city's rooftops, clearing away icicles before they can crash down on unsuspecting pedestrians.

To combat the cold, Muscovites wear layers of warm coats and sweaters. Traditional fur hats have flaps to cover the ears. Despite the brutal cold, winter offers many pleasures. Children and grown-ups enjoy ice skating, sledding, and making sparkling sculptures out of snow.

As the days grow longer and warmer, Moscow comes to life fully. People gather in the parks to have picnics, play chess, or simply to delight in the sunshine. During the summer, it is best to carry an umbrella. Sudden, intense downpours are frequent, turning the streets to rivers in a matter of moments.

Moscow summers do not last long. In September, the days grow chilly and the nights are cold. By October, Muscovites get out their heavy coats and fur hats again, in time for the first snowfall.

*This traditional fur hat complete with ear flaps for those bitter Moscow winters carries the Enlisted Man's ensign on the front.*

During the Middle Ages, monks in present-day Russia kept careful records about people and events. One such account states that on April 4, 1147, a prince named Yuri Dolgoruki gave a splendid banquet to cement a new political alliance. The banquet was held at the prince's castle on the Moskva River. This castle stood somewhere on the site of present-day Moscow. This story is the earliest written reference to the city. Though the spot had been inhabited for hundreds of years, Russian schoolchildren are taught that 1147 is the year of Moscow's founding.

*Yuri Dolgoruki* (YOO-ree DULL-GAH-ROO-kee)

# SAFE BEHIND THE WALLS

In Prince Yuri Dolgoruki's time, the land we call Russia was made up of many small warring states. The Russians fought among themselves, and were constantly harassed by the Tartars, a nomadic people from central Asia. No settlement was safe from enemy attack. In 1156, the rulers of Moscow ordered the construction of a fort with thick earthen walls. The walls were topped by ramparts made from heavy logs. This primitive fort was the ancestor of today's Kremlin.

The city of Moscow rose on a broad plain dotted with gentle hills. It soon became a lively center for trade. Merchants shipped goods into the city along the Moskva River. Caravans of packhorses brought silks, ivory, and other trade goods across the plains from the east.

Sometimes, invading armies also swept over the plain. In 1238, Moscow and much of the surrounding territory fell to the Tartars. Tartar rule brought many hardships for the people of Moscow. After two hundred years, several Moscow princes organized an uprising that overthrew the invaders.

*Left: Seventeenth-century Russian imperial and ecclesiastical costumes*
*Below: Russian Tartars*

In 1367, a stone castle replaced Moscow's earth and log fortress. Over the years, a series of walls were built around the city. Here and there along the walls stood "defensive monasteries." These monasteries were places of spiritual retreat for the monks who lived there. But they were also outposts for soldiers who guarded the city.

As Moscow grew more powerful, it gained greater control of the surrounding territory. Its princes ruled an ever-expanding empire. In 1547, Ivan IV (known to history as Ivan the Terrible) was crowned tsar of all Russia. The capital of this vast empire was the city of Moscow.

*Left: Ivan IV*
*(Ivan the Terrible)*

*Tartar* (TAR-TER)
*Ivan* (EE-VAHN)

# Terror in the Kremlin
Like many emperors before and since, Ivan IV of Russia (1530–1584) executed thousands of innocent people. In a fit of rage, he even killed his own son. But his horrible deeds earned him a lasting nickname. He is still remembered as Ivan the Terrible.

# THE ABANDONED CAPITAL

The tsars of Russia lured some of Europe's greatest architects to Moscow. These masters designed cathedrals and palaces blending Italian and Russian features. From a boat on the river, the city offered a stunning panorama of domes and spires. Moscow became a magnet for artists, musicians, and scholars from all over Russia. But despite its buildings and its culture, Moscow was not a European city. The great European capitals—Rome, Paris, London—were unimaginably far away. European travelers seldom reached Moscow, and Muscovites seemed to turn inward. The city had only a handful of schools, and few people knew how to read and write.

Tsar Peter I (Peter the Great) longed for Russia to take its place among the cultured nations of the world. He felt that Russians should begin to look outward, toward the vital cities of western Europe. In 1712, he shifted the Russian capital from Moscow to St. Petersburg on the Gulf of Finland. Unlike Moscow, St. Petersburg was a port city, bustling with activity. By comparison, Moscow seemed isolated and remote.

*Tsar Peter I (Peter the Great)*

*Moscow, about 1738*

*When Napoleon Bonaparte won the 1812 Battle of*
*Borodino (above), Moscow fell into enemy hands.*

Moscow lost some of its glitter when it gave up its status as the capital. But it remained a beautiful city, an island of culture on the vast Russian plain. When French emperor Napoleon Bonaparte invaded Russia, Moscow was his goal. In 1812, Napoleon's army marched across the plains and attacked the city. Just outside Moscow, Napoleon met the Russian forces at the Battle of Borodino. Both sides suffered terrible losses, but when the battle was over, Moscow was in enemy hands.

> *Napolean Bonaparte* (NUH-POLE-EE-UN BONE-UH-PART)
> *Borodino* (BAH-ROH-DEE-NUH)

As the French troops poured through the city gates, Muscovites fled for their lives. Soon, the city was nearly abandoned, left to the invading soldiers. But the Muscovites could not bear to think of enemies enjoying their beloved city. Before they departed, many set fire to their homes and shops. Other fires flared up, perhaps set by the soldiers as they looted empty buildings. Within days, Moscow was a seething inferno. Small, scattered blazes converged into one disastrous conflagration. Flames engulfed block after block. No safe corner remained. The French had captured the city, but as they watched, their prize turned to ashes.

After only a few weeks, Napoleon withdrew from the devastated city. As he and his soldiers recrossed the plains, they were overtaken by one of the harshest winters in Russia's history. Thousands of troops died of cold, hunger, and disease.

Gradually, the Muscovites returned and began the daunting task of rebuilding their city. They

built new houses and restored once-glorious churches and palaces. As the years passed, the last traces of the great fire disappeared. Once again, Moscow stood splendid and strong. The

rebuilding of Moscow is still regarded as one of the proudest moments in Russian history.

*Above: Only a few weeks after capturing Moscow, Napoleon retreated from the burning city.*

*Above: An early view of the Kremlin*

*Left: An 1892 court ball*

# THE POWER OF THE PEOPLE

In the era of the tsars, the Russian nobles lived in luxury. They dined on the finest foods and rode through the streets in elegant carriages. They had the power of life and death over the peasants who worked on their huge estates.

In 1905, a group of angry workers, students, and soldiers tried to overthrow the tsar. These revolutionaries were inspired by a German philosopher named Karl Marx. Marx believed that a new system called Communism could break the power of the rich and elevate the working classes. The revolution of 1905 was unsuccessful. But in 1917, Communist forces under Vladimir Lenin deposed Tsar Nicholas II.

*Tsar bank notes*

Russia became the world's first Communist nation. The following year, the Communist government made Moscow the capital once more. Over the next two decades, fifteen neighboring states were drawn together within the Union of Soviet Socialist Republics, or USSR.

The Communists seized the property of the wealthy nobles. In Moscow, they took control of the stores and factories. Profits from these state-run businesses went to the government, while the workers earned pitifully low wages. Despite the promises of the revolution, life did not improve for the Russian people.

*Vladimir Lenin, under whose leadership Communist forces deposed Tsar Nicholas II in 1917*

*Above: The new tsar, Nicholas II, kisses his mother after his coronation in 1894*

*Vladimir Lenin* (VLAD-IH-MEER LEH-NINN)
*Tsar Nicholas* (TSAHR NICK-OH-LUSS)

During the 1930s and 1940s, Soviet leader Josef Stalin launched a disastrous series of "purges" against his enemies, both real and imagined. Millions of Russians, including tens of thousands of Muscovites, died during Stalin's reign of terror. The situation grew even more desperate with the outbreak of World War II. In 1941, German troops swept into Russia. They came within sight of the Kremlin's towers before Soviet forces finally drove them back. In the course of the war, some 20 million Russians lost their lives.

*Left: A World War II Soviet medal*
*Below: Soviet leader Josef Stalin (front row, second from left) with members of the Politburo (the Communist executive committee)*

In the decades after World War II, Muscovites struggled to rebuild their city and their lives. Most people had jobs, but food and other goods were scarce. People stood in long lines to buy necessities such as milk, eggs, and butter. Few people dared to criticize the government. Enemies of the state were still in severe jeopardy.

In 1985, Mikhail Gorbachev became the new Soviet leader. Gorbachev tried to reform the Communist system by allowing some free trade and greater freedom of speech. This era of new freedom was known in Russian as *perestroika*. Some Russians were dismayed by the sudden changes. Others felt that Gorbachev's reforms did not go far enough. They wanted to dismantle the Communist government altogether.

*Above: German stukas (dive-bomber airplanes) raiding Moscow during World War II in July 1941*
*Right: In 1985, the new Soviet leader Mikhail Gorbachev instituted* perestroika, *an era of new freedom in the Soviet Union.*

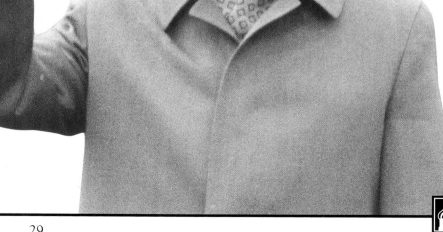

*Josef Stalin* (JOH-seff STAH-linn)
*Mikhail Gorbachev* (MEE-KHAH-EEL guhr-bah-CHYOFF)
*perestroika* (PEH-REH-STROY-kuh)

Tensions exploded in August 1991, when old-guard Communists staged a coup against Premier Gorbachev. The rebels attempted to take over the parliament building, known as the White House. Crowds of demonstrators filled the streets, shouting their support of Gorbachev's reforms. At this critical point, parliamentary president Boris Yeltsin clambered atop an armored tank and gave an impassioned speech. He called on the demonstrators to protect the parliament, even to give their lives for the cause of freedom. The demonstrators held their ground, even when rebel tanks threatened to mow them down.

Though the 1991 coup failed, it signaled the end of Communism in the Soviet Union. In December 1991, Mikhail Gorbachev resigned, and the Communist system collapsed. One by one, the neighboring republics broke away from Russia. The people of Moscow waited with tension and hope to learn what the future would hold.

*Parliamentary president Boris Yeltsin (front row, fourth from left, in brown suit) changed the course of the Soviet Union when his impassioned speech convinced his countrymen to rethink their commitment to Communism.*

*Boris Yeltsin*
(BOHR-ISS YELT-SINN)
*Oprichnina*
(UH-PREECH-NEE-NUH)

## Somebody's Watching!

In 1565, Ivan the Terrible founded a group of 1,000 mounted soldiers called the Oprichnina. They rode throughout the countryside, seizing property from the tsar's rivals and executing anyone who stood in their way. Like the Oprichnina, Stalin's secret police of the 1930s (the KGB) also spread terror among the Russian people. Moscow and the rest of the Soviet Union lived in fear of the KGB, which arrested anyone suspected of disloyalty. The KGB was finally disbanded in 1993.

*Left: Mikhail Gorbachev*

*Right: A KGB badge*

There is a myth that the Muscovite character is dark and somber, cold as a January wind off the Moskva. But the people of Moscow, like people everywhere, have endless facets. They can be deeply serious, but they also love to have fun. Muscovites excel in the realms of music, drama, dance, and athletics. The city has produced some of the greatest writers in the world. Before you decide about the Muscovite character, you must look at Moscow's achievements in entertainment and the arts.

# ON WITH THE SHOW!

**M**uscovites adore circuses. They love to cheer for lion tamers, bareback riders, and fearless masters of the high-wire. The antics of painted clowns make them roar with laughter. With headquarters on the city's Tsvetnoi (Colorful) Boulevard, the Moscow Circus is one of the finest in the world. It recruits the best performers in all of Russia.

The circus is not the only show that draws crowds in Moscow. Muscovites follow ballet with passionate devotion. The Bolshoi Theater, founded in 1824, hosts Moscow's world-famous Bolshoi Ballet Company.

During the nineteenth century, the Bolshoi trained orphans to be dancers. In 1887, the company premiered *Swan Lake*, a magnificent ballet by Russian composer Peter Ilych Tchaikovsky. During the 1930s, political leaders often gave long speeches from the stage of the Bolshoi. Audiences would sit patiently through a two-hour harangue for the sake of the ballet that followed. Today, the Bolshoi Ballet makes frequent tours to major cities around the world. In addition to ballet, the Bolshoi Theater presents several operas each year.

*Below: Clowns in the Moscow Circus wear bow ties like this one and use multicolored face paint.*

Top left and right: Moscow
Circus performers

Left: Bolshoi Ballet dancers

Tsvetnoi (TVYETT-NOY)
Bolshoi (BAHL-SHOY)
Peter Ilych Tchaikovsky
(PEET-EHR EEL-YEECH CHY-KAWF-SKEE)

The Bolshoi (meaning "big") is one of three theaters on Moscow's Theater Square. The others are the Maly (meaning "little") and the Children's Theater. Another theater with a remarkable history is the Moscow Arts Theater, founded in 1898 by the famous director Konstantin Stanislavsky. Stanislavsky taught actors the value of "getting in character" when they studied a role. He felt it was more important for the actor to understand the character's feelings than to memorize lines. The Moscow Art Theater gave the first performances of *The Three Sisters*, *The Cherry Orchard*, and other plays by Anton Chekhov. Chekhov came to Moscow from southern Russia in 1879 to study medicine. While practicing as a doctor, he wrote and published short stories. He once told a friend, "Medicine is my lawful wife, but literature is my mistress."

The Tchaikovsky Concert Hall honors the memory of Russia's foremost classical composer. The concert hall is home base for the Moscow State Symphony, as well as a dance company and a choral ensemble. But you

*Arbat* (ARR-BAHT)
*Maly* (MAHL-uy)
*Konstantin Stanislavsky*
(KUNN-STAHN-TEEN STAH-NEE-SLAV-SKEE)
*Anton Chekhov* (ANN-TOHN CHECK-OFF)
*balalaika* (BUH-LAH-LY-KUH)
*Luzhniki* (LOOZH-NEE-KEE)
*Afghanistan* (AFF-GAN-IH-STAN)

*The Bolshoi Theater*

don't have to go to the concert hall to hear good music. On summer days, many young musicians give impromptu performances in Moscow's parks. Muscovites love to hear the strains of a flute or violin as they wander among the trees. Now and then, someone strums the balalaika, a stringed instrument with a soft, plaintive tone.

Athletic performance is another form of showmanship in Moscow. In 1980, the city hosted the Summer Olympic Games. To prepare for this event, Moscow expanded Luzhniki (Meadow) Stadium, originally built in 1956. The stadium now has a whopping seating capacity of 103,000. It could easily hold the entire population of a city such as Albany, New York, or Berkeley, California. In the summer, Luzhniki Stadium hosts soccer matches. Ice hockey is the major draw during the winter months. The stadium is part of a sprawling sports complex with swimming pools, tennis courts, and arenas.

*Musicians entertain on Arbat Street*

## Sports and Politics

The 1980 Olympics in Moscow brought together teams of elite athletes from all over the globe. But the United States did not take part in the games. The Soviet Union had recently invaded the nation of Afghanistan, and the United States withdrew from the games as a gesture of protest. Moscow's Olympic Village covered 250 acres (101 hectares) and is now the site of the Luzhniki Sports Complex.

# STORIES OF A PEOPLE

Russia is an enormous country, the largest in the world. It is only fitting that it has produced literature of titanic stature. Many of Russia's finest writers have lived and worked in Moscow. Like Chekhov, Mikhail Bulgakov (1891–1940) began his career as a physician. In the 1920s, he delighted readers with his humorous political satires. Soviet authorities, however, were not amused. Bulgakov was forbidden to write, and by the time he died, his work was nearly forgotten. In 1967, however, his masterpiece, *The Master and Margarita,* was published in English. Twenty-seven years after his death, Bulgakov received the international praise he deserved.

In contrast, Maxim Gorky (1868–1936) was embraced by the Comunist authorities as a writer who carried the "correct" political message. Gorky wrote about his impoverished childhood, and recounted the wretched lives of tramps and outcasts.

Moscow is the setting for much of Boris Pasternak's unforgettable novel *Doctor Zhivago.* Because his work criticized the 1917 revolution and its aftermath, Pasternak (1890–1960) had serious problems with the authorities. *Doctor Zhivago* was never published in the Soviet Union during Pasternak's lifetime. But the manuscript was smuggled into Italy, where it was published in 1957. Boris Pasternak was awarded the Nobel Prize for literature in 1958. Fearing for his safety and that of his family, he refused to travel to Sweden to accept the most prestigious literary prize in the world. His son accepted the prize on his behalf in 1992.

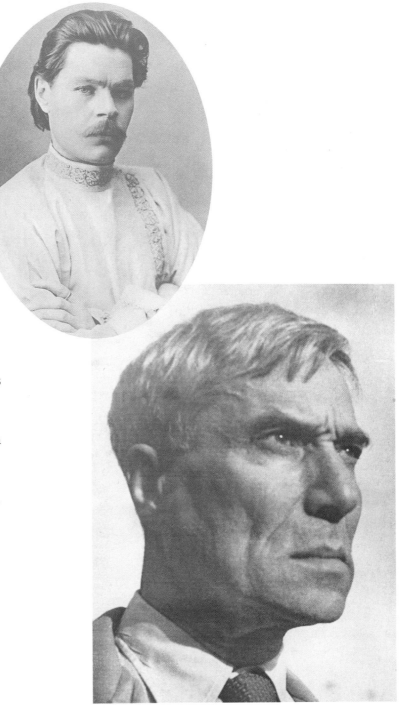

*Top: Maxim Gorky*
*Right: Boris Pasternak*

Of all Russia's writers, none is more revered than Leo Tolstoy (1828–1910). Tolstoy grew up on an estate some 170 miles (274 km) from Moscow. But he also maintained a home in Moscow for many years. Tolstoy's two greatest novels are *War and Peace* (1869) and *Anna Karenina* (1877). Tolstoy is remembered not only as a novelist, but also as a social reformer. Though he was born to the nobility, he had compassion for the poor, and even started a school for peasant children. To this day, young people in Russia are inspired by Tolstoy's quest for spiritual meaning. His last words were, "To seek. Always to seek."

*Anna Karenina (right) is one of the great novels written by Leo Tolstoy (above).*

*Mikhail Bulgakov* (MEE-KAH-EEL BOOL-GAH-KOFF)
*Maxim Gorky* (MAHK-SEEM GOHR-KEE)
*Boris Pasternak* (BOHR-ISS PASS-TER-NACK)
*Zhivago* (ZHEE-VAH-GO)
*Leo Tolstoy* (LEE-OH TOLL-STOY)
*Anna Karenina* (ANN-UH KUH-REH-NIN-UH)

# THE ARTIST'S WAY

During the years of Communist rule, the Soviet government supported the arts in Moscow. The government commissioned murals to decorate public buildings. Paintings and statues adorned Metro stations. Large outdoor sculptures sprang up in every city park. The purpose of all this artwork was to celebrate the Communist system and its leaders. The government kept plenty of artists busy, but for the most part their paintings and sculptures lacked feeling. True art was lost behind a relentless political message.

After 1991, Moscow artists were free to express themselves. The fall of Communism brought an explosion of artistic activity. Political posters and murals disappeared, replaced by

*An artist painting on the grounds of a museum in Kolomenskoye*

*Kolomenskoye*
(KAH-LOH-MYENN-SKOH-YE)

modernistic abstracts or scenes of everyday life. Many artists even dared to satirize the old Communist statues and paintings. The face of Lenin appeared in clownish poses, or grinned from carved wooden dolls.

In the pre-revolution era, wealthy Muscovites collected art objects from western Europe. These private collections were confiscated in 1917. Some of these paintings were displayed in museums, gifts to the public from the new government. Others were locked away out of sight.

In 1953, a few weeks after Stalin's death, a small group of high Communist officials entered a back room of the Pushkin Fine Arts Museum. There they viewed a collection of works by Matisse, Picasso, and other French impressionists. No one had been allowed to look at these pictures since Stalin came to power. Today, they are proudly on exhibit at the Pushkin Museum.

*Top: An artist trying to sell his caricature of Mikhail Gorbachev*

*Right: A painter on a high perch restores frescoes on the ceiling of St. Basil's Cathedral.*

*Pushkin* (POOSH-keen)

The Tretyakov Gallery features many more "lost" paintings. It has an extensive collection of works by Russian artists and painters from western Europe. The Tretyakov is the largest and most respected art museum in Moscow.

Among the finest examples of Russian art to be seen in Moscow are the icons created for Eastern Orthodox churches. Icons are paintings on wood panels and are based on sacred themes. Some depict scenes from the life of Christ. Others represent saints or angels. The *iconostasis* is a screen at the front of the church, covered with paintings of Biblical scenes.

Thousands of beautiful icons were destroyed during the Communist era. Others were preserved as museum pieces. In the 1990s, as Moscow churches reopened for worship, icons were allowed to serve as sacred images once again.

*The Tretyakov Gallery*

*Tretyakov* (TREET-YAH-KOFF)
*iconostasis* (IGH-KUH-NAH-STUH-SISS)
*Andrei Rublyov* (AHN-DRAY ROOB-LY-OFF)

*Left: Religious icons in St. Basil's Cathedral*

# Moscow's Mystery Painter

Andrei Rublyov (1360–1430) is regarded as the greatest icon painter in the history of Russia. Yet almost nothing is known about his life. It is not even certain which icons he painted himself. During Rublyov's lifetime, Russian painters did not sign their work. Scholars must search for evidence in church records and other documents of the day. Such evidence proves that Rublyov painted *The Old Testament Trinity*, which now hangs in the Tretyakov Gallery.

One of the best ways to view Moscow is from the deck of a boat on the Moskva River. The river twists and curves through the city, taking visitors from the quiet outskirts to the teeming center of government and culture. To experience Moscow close up, however, you need to take the buses, ride the Metro, and walk the streets. You should visit museums and churches, sit in the park, take in a soccer match, or try the ballet. Little by little, you may get to know the fascinating city that is Moscow.

# OUT ON THE EDGE

Over the centuries, Moscow grew out from the center. High-rise apartment buildings and rumbling factories stand in many of the outlying neighborhoods. Such neighborhoods are made more livable by small, wedge-shaped parks scattered among the high-rise towers. Here and there, wooded tracts have been preserved, even within the city limits. Moscow is ringed by a "green belt," a series of parks and forests that cover some 695 square miles (1,800 sq km).

One of Moscow's southeastern suburbs is the former village of Kolomenskoye. Kolomenskoye was once a summer retreat of the tsars and nobles. The ornate Kazan Cathedral was built in the late seventeenth century. Wooden houses and farm buildings from many parts of Russia have been transported to a park surrounding the church.

The Sparrow Hills section, in southwestern Moscow, is an oasis of peace amid the city's modern bustle. Known as "Lenin Hills" from 1924 until 1992, this area has extensive parkland devoted to recreation. In the short summer months, the hills lure hikers and picnickers. In winter, skiers

*Left: A Kolomenskoye woman in traditional dress*
*Below: Muscovites enjoying a Sunday afternoon in Pushkin Square, one of Moscow's many parks*

and tobogganers swoop down the snow-covered slopes.

Luzhniki Stadium and its surrounding sports complex is a major attraction of the Sparrow Hills neighborhood. In front of the stadium is a lively flea market, where you can find anything from ironing boards to balalaikas.

A major landmark of Sparrow Hills is the "wedding-cake tower" of Moscow State University. Founded in 1755, the university has an enrollment of 28,000. Students live in tiny, sparsely furnished rooms. Yet few complain about the accommodations. To attend the university is considered a great privilege.

*Above: The "wedding-cake tower" of Moscow State University*

*Kazan* (KAH-ZAHN)

47

# WITHIN THE GARDEN RING

The highway known as the Garden Ring follows the line of a medieval wall that once protected the city. The Garden Ring marks Moscow's outer rim. Another beltway, the Boulevard Ring, traces the wall that once encircled the Kremlin. Between the Garden Ring and the Boulevard Ring spreads a web of streets, dotted with major landmarks and hidden surprises.

Until the 1300s, the section called Kitay-Gorod was a separate walled village. Parts of its original wall still stand near the Russia Hotel. Completed in 1971, the Russia boasts 6,000 rooms, making it the biggest hotel in the world. It is such a maze of stairways and branching corridors that guests often get lost.

Kitay-Gorod was once the merchants' quarter of Moscow. The famous Merchants Yard was designed by an Italian architect named Giacomo Guarenghi, and opened in 1805. Today, this magnificent arcade is used for shops and offices.

*A Russian folk doll*

Kitay-Gorod (KEE-TY-GO-RUDD)
Lubyanka (LOO-BYAN-KUH)
Felix Dzerzhinsky
(FYEH-LEEKS DYAIR-ZHEEN-SKEE)

Lubyanka Square was once the site of KGB headquarters. Until 1991, the square bore the name of secret police founder Felix Dzerzhinsky. The statue of "Iron Felix" was a prominent landmark. Today, Iron Felix is gone. In its place stands a cross in memory of the thousands of people who died at Dzerzhinsky's hands.

An old Russian saying states that "Children are the only privileged class in our country." A visit to the Children's Store off Lubyanka Square is all the proof one needs. The store overflows with costumed dolls, musical instruments, puzzles, toy soldiers, and electronic games.

*According to Russians, children are the only privileged class in their country. Shown here are a toddler in the arms of her father (top) and preschool children in an English class (left).*

The Arbat is one of the most charming areas of Moscow. It was once the home of such writers as Pushkin, Tolstoy, Bulgakov, and Pasternak. Arbat Street, the main thoroughfare, is a pedestrian walkway lined with enticing shops. In spring and summer, the Arbat is alive with mimes, jugglers, artists, vendors, and street musicians. Elegant mansions, now broken into apartments, still stand on many side streets.

Red Square, Moscow's central plaza, was once the city's main marketplace. The name comes from the Russian word *krasnuiy*, which means both "red" and "beautiful." Muscovites gather at Red Square for parades, festivals, and political rallies. Even on an ordinary day, Red Square is crowded with people.

Some of Moscow's most spectacular buildings front Red Square. The Kazan Cathedral was dedicated in 1636 and

*Kazan Cathedral*

*krasnuiy* (KRAHS-nuy)
*Basil* (BAZZ-ill)

demolished three centuries later by the Communists. Following the original design, the cathedral was reconstructed in the 1980s. The splendid St. Basil's Cathedral, with its crown of domes and towers, is one of Moscow's best-known landmarks. Another building on the square is the handsome red brick Moscow Historical Museum. With a vast collection of 4 million items, the museum captures the story of Russia from ancient times to the present. Among the museum's greatest treasures are Peter the Great's sleigh, Napoleon's saber, and the royal wardrobe of Ivan the Terrible.

The western side of Red Square lies along the eastern wall of the Kremlin. Nestled against the wall is a marble mausoleum housing the body of revolutionary leader Vladimir Lenin. People still travel from all over Russia to pay their respects at this national shrine. Lenin's embalmed body is on full view in a glass case. A team of thirteen doctors is assigned the task of checking the body and keeping it in shape.

*A guard at Lenin's Tomb on Red Square*

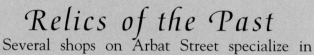

# Relics of the Past

Several shops on Arbat Street specialize in memorabilia from the Communist era. You can buy old political posters, surplus Army fatigues, and statues of Communist leaders. Once, portraits of Lenin and other figures were seen everywhere in Moscow. Today, such pictures are collectibles, relics of a bygone era.

# BEHIND THE KREMLIN WALLS

For nearly 700 years, the Kremlin has been the heart of Moscow. Many of the Kremlin's palaces and churches are closed to the public, their treasures hidden behind locked doors. Even so, 60,000 visitors walk the halls and courtyards of the Kremlin each day, eager to see all that can be seen.

The Kremlin grew, piece by piece, over the centuries, without any systematic plan. One example of this hodgepodge growth is the Great Kremlin Palace. Completed in 1849, the Kremlin Palace was built over and around several smaller palaces. Inside, it is a jumble of architectural styles. The centerpiece of the palace is St. George's Hall, an immense, echoing chamber with a vaulted ceiling 58 feet (18 meters) high.

Another remarkable Kremlin sight is the Palace of Facets, completed under Tsar Ivan III in 1491. The walls of its Great Chamber are adorned with stunning religious paintings. In this hall, Ivan the Terrible celebrated his victory over the Tartars in 1551.

For those who love military history, the Armory is endlessly fascinating. This museum holds an extensive collection of weapons and armor dating as far back as the 1500s. Other sections of the Armory include the royal stables, with an array of elaborate saddles and harnesses; and the royal sewing room, with the wardrobes of several tsars and tsarinas. Among the other displays are the tsars' jewelry, several imperial carriages, and Ivan the Terrible's ornately carved throne.

The Palace of Congresses is the newest palace in the Kremlin. Its

*A view of the Kremlin with the Moskva River in the foreground*

vast main hall can seat 6,000 people. Built in the 1950s, the palace served as headquarters for the Soviet parliament. Today, Russia's parliament meets in the White House, an unassuming building across the river.

*Above: An ornate imperial carriage in the Armory Museum*
*Below: Russian schoolgirls*

# The Red Staircase

Leading from the Palace of Facets is the magnificent Red Staircase. During weddings, christenings, and other religious ceremonies, royal processions once descended these stairs to reach the Cathedral of the Annunciation. Napoleon stood on the staircase in 1812 and watched fire devour much of Moscow. The staircase was destroyed during the 1930s but was rebuilt in 1994.

*The tsars used Annunciation Cathedral (on the left in this picture) for weddings, christenings, and private worship. The Bell Tower of Ivan the Great (on the right), named for Saint Ivan, is the tallest structure in the Kremlin.*

For people around the world, St. Basil's Cathedral (left) has become the symbol of Russia.

Below: A Moscow schoolgirl at St. Basil's Cathedral

By long tradition, Russian tsars were crowned in the Cathedral of the Assumption. Much of this cathedral's original artwork has been destroyed or moved to museums. But the building remains a marvel, conveying a sense of power and immensity.

The tsars used the Cathedral of the Annunciation for weddings, christenings, and private worship. On its walls are glorious frescoes of Biblical scenes and the Holy Family. Ivan the Terrible added several domes and ordered the whole roof to be covered with gold.

The Bell Tower of Ivan the Great was named for Russia's Saint Ivan, and not for one of the tsars. Standing 257 feet (78 m) tall, it is the highest structure in the Kremlin. Twenty-one bells once hung in its belfry. The huge Resurrection Bell used to toll three times to announce the death of a tsar.

The chimes that sound the hour in Moscow do not ring from the Bell Tower. They float from the Kremlin's Savior Tower and are broadcast all over Russia. The chimes remind the Russian people that Moscow is the vital center of their great and ever-changing nation.

# FAMOUS LANDMARKS

*Above: The Moscow Historical Museum*

*Right: St. Basil's Cathedral domes*

*Right: A view of Red Square*

**Luzhniki Stadium**
Originally built in the 1950s, this stadium was expanded for the 1980 Olympics in Moscow. It now seats 103,000 spectators. The stadium is the center of a sports complex with tennis courts, swimming pools, and arenas.

**Russia Hotel**
Containing 6,000 rooms for guests, the Russia is the biggest hotel in the world. Many consider this hulking modern structure to be a Moscow eyesore.

**Red Square**
Moscow's central plaza, the square is the site of public rallies and ceremonies. It is also a place where Muscovites gather for fun and entertainment.

**Kazan Cathedral**
This famous Eastern Orthodox cathedral was dedicated in 1636. In 1936, it was destroyed by the Communists under Stalin. The cathedral was fully rebuilt and reopened in the 1980s.

**Moscow Historical Museum**
This brick building on Red Square is a treasure-house of items from Russia's long and varied history. All of Russia's numerous ethnic groups are represented. The museum's prizes include Napoleon's saber and field kitchen, and clothing worn by Ivan the Terrible.

**St. Basil's Cathedral**
Commissioned by Ivan the Terrible, this splendid cathedral was completed in 1560. It was named in honor of Holy Basil the Fool, one of the tsar's few outspoken critics. The cathedral is crowned with gables, pinnacles, and onion-shaped domes.

**Museum of Applied Folk Arts**
In this museum a visitor can view fascinating collections of weavings, ceramics, carvings, and other crafts from every part of the former Soviet Union.

One room displays some 150 elaborate samovars, or Russian tea urns, some dating back to the 1700s.

**Palace of the Sixteenth and Seventeenth Centuries in Zaryadye**
Originally, this elaborate building was a palace of Russia's tsars. Today, it is a historical museum. On exhibit are period clothing and furniture, as well as a noble's fully restored study. Parts of a seventeenth-century monastery can also be seen, including the barren cells where the monks once lived.

Below: The Kremlin Palace (left) with Annunciation Cathedral and the Bell Tower of Ivan the Great (right)

Above: Cathedral of Christ the Savior

## Tretyakov Gallery

This art museum contains many priceless works confiscated from private collections after the 1917 revolution. It is the largest art museum in Moscow. The Tretyakov features paintings and sculptures by Russian artists.

## Pushkin Fine Arts Museum

Named for the Russian poet Alexander Pushkin, this museum is noted for its collection of paintings by Matisse, Picasso, and other impressionists.

## Museum of the Revolution

The troubled history of twentieth-century Russia is recounted in this museum. Documents, photos, and other displays recall the revolution of 1917, which established Communism; and the revolution of 1991, which brought it to an end. Attempted revolts in 1905 and 1993 are also represented.

## Theater Square

Three theaters surround this square: the Children's Theater, the Maly (Little), and the Bolshoi (Big). The Bolshoi is home to Moscow's world-famous Bolshoi Ballet Company. It also hosts opera performances.

## Tolstoy Estate Museum

Novelist Leo Tolstoy spent his summers in this house between 1882 and 1901. The house, barn, and other outbuildings have been restored to show how a noble Russian family lived in the late nineteenth century. The study contains Tolstoy's original desk, complete with pens, ink, and paperweights. Some of Tolstoy's possessions hint at his eccentric lifestyle. In his study are a bicycle, a set of weights, and an array of shoemaking tools.

## Cathedral of Christ the Savior

This enormous cathedral, completed in 1883, was destroyed by Stalin in 1931. It was rebuilt during the 1990s according to the original design. The largest cathedral in Russia, it has five gilded domes, one soaring 300 feet (91 m) into the sky.

## Great Kremlin Palace

Completed in 1849, this palace absorbed several smaller palaces within the Kremlin walls. Its central chamber, St. George's Hall, is 60 feet (18 m) wide, 200 feet (61 m) long, and 58 feet (18 m) high.

## Bell Tower of Ivan the Great

At 257 feet (84 m), this tower is the tallest structure in the Kremlin. Twenty-one great bells once tolled from its belfry. The famous Tsar's Bell rests at the foot of the tower. Cast in 1735, it cracked two years later when doused with cold water during a fire. The Tsar's Bell is 21 feet (6.4 m) in diameter and weighs 230 tons (207 metric tons).

# FAST FACTS

## POPULATION

| | |
|---|---|
| City | 7,801,000 |
| Metropolitan Area | 8,957,000 (1995) |

## AREA

339 square miles (879 square kilometers)

## LOCATION
Moscow lies on a series of low hills on the plains of northwestern Russia. The Moskva River loops through the city. The Moskva is a tributary of the Oka, which in turn feeds the Volga. Moscow is the capital of the Republic of Russia.

## CLIMATE
Moscow is famous for its long cold winters. January temperatures average 15 degrees Fahrenheit (–9.4° Celsius). Summers are brief, with frequent downpours. The average July temperature is 65 degrees Fahrenheit (18° Celsius).

## ECONOMY
As Moscow is the national capital, the government is a major employer. The city also has many factories. Some businesses are run by the state, while others are now private. Moscow factories make automobiles, chemical products, steel, textiles, electrical machinery, and processed foods.

# CHRONOLOGY

### 1147
Prince Yuri Dolgoruki hosts a banquet at his castle on the Moskva River; this is the earliest written reference to the city of Moscow.

### 1156
A fort of earth and timber is constructed at the site of today's Kremlin.

### 1238
Moscow falls to the Tartars of central Asia.

### 1367
A stone fortress replaces Moscow's earlier fort.

### 1547
Ivan IV (known as Ivan the Terrible) is crowned tsar of all Russia.

### 1712
Tsar Peter the Great moves the Russian capital from Moscow to St. Petersburg.

### 1812
Napoleon Bonaparte invades Moscow but retreats when the city is swept by fire.

### 1905
Revolutionaries try unsuccessfully to overthrow the tsar.

### 1917
A successful revolution overthrows the tsar and establishes a Communist government.

*A misty view of the Kremlin reflected in the Moskva River*

**1918**
The Russian capital moves back to Moscow.

**1937–1939**
Josef Stalin launches a deadly series of "purges" against his enemies.

**1939–1945**
Some 20 million Russians die in the Second World War.

**1958**
Fearing for his life, Boris Pasternak refuses to travel to Sweden to accept the Nobel Prize for literature.

**1980**
Moscow hosts the Olympic Games.

**1985**
Mikhail Gorbachev becomes Russia's leader and ushers in an era of openness known as *perestroika*.

**1991**
Rebels try to overthrow Gorbachev's government; Gorbachev resigns; and the Communist system collapses in Russia.

**1996**
Yuri Luzhkov, known as a man who gets things done, is overwhelmingly elected to serve as Moscow's mayor.

# MOSCOW

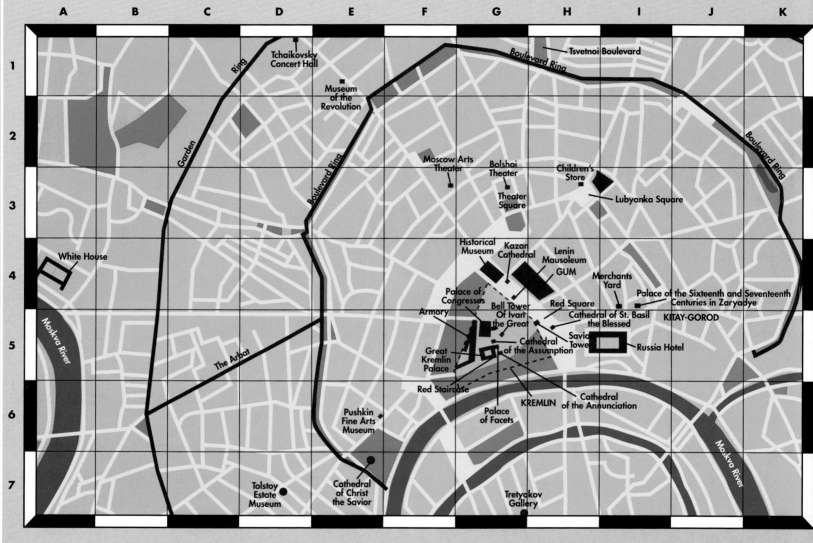

Tchaikovsky Concert Hall

Tsvetnoi Boulevard

Boulevard Ring

Garden Ring

Museum of the Revolution

Moscow Arts Theater

Bolshoi Theater

Theater Square

Children's Store

Lubyanka Square

White House

Historical Museum

Kazan Cathedral

Lenin Mausoleum

GUM

Merchants Yard

Palace of the Sixteenth and Seventeenth Centuries in Zaryadye

Palace of Congresses

Bell Tower Of Ivan the Great

Armory

Red Square

Cathedral of St. Basil the Blessed

KITAY-GOROD

Moskva River

The Arbat

Great Kremlin Palace

Cathedral of the Assumption

Savior Tower

Russia Hotel

Red Staircase

KREMLIN

Cathedral of the Annunciation

Palace of Facets

Pushkin Fine Arts Museum

Moskva River

Tolstoy Estate Museum

Cathedral of Christ the Savior

Tretyakov Gallery

| | | | | | |
|---|---|---|---|---|---|
| The Arbat | B-D 5,6 | Children's Store | H3 | Lubyanka Square | H3 |
| Armory | G5 | Garden Ring | M-N 2,3 | Luzhniki Stadium | M3 |
| Bell Tower of Ivan the Great | G5 | Great Kremlin Palace | G5 | Merchants Yard | I4 |
| Bolshoi Theater | G3 | GUM | G-H 4 | Moscow | L-O 1-4 |
| Borodino Museum | M3 | Historical Museum | G4 | Moscow State University | M3 |
| Boulevard Ring | N 2,3 | Kazan Cathedral | G4 | Moscow Arts Theater | F3 |
| Cathedral of the Annunciation | G5 | Kitay-Gorod | I-J 4,5 | Moskva River | A 4-7; F-K 5-7 |
| Cathedral of the Assumption | G5 | Kolomenskoye | O4 | Museum of the Revolution | E1 |
| Cathedral of Christ the Savior | E7 | Kremlin | G-H 4-6 | Museum of Applied Folk Art | N2 |
| Cathedral of St. Basil the Blessed | H5 | Lenin Mausoleum | G4 | Palace of Facets | G5 |

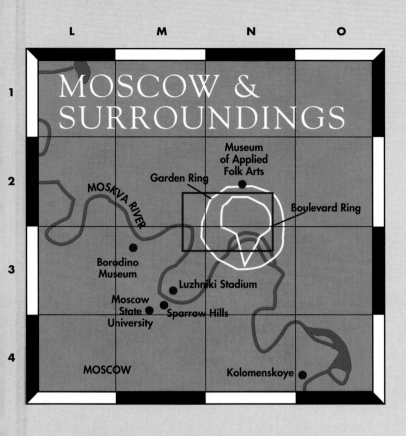

MOSCOW & SURROUNDINGS

| | |
|---|---|
| Palace of Congresses | G5 |
| Palace of the Sixteenth and Seventeenth Centuries in Zaryadye | I4 |
| Pushkin Fine Arts Museum | E-F 6 |
| Red Square | G-H 4,5 |
| Red Staircase | G5 |
| Russia Hotel | H-I 5 |
| Savior Tower | H5 |
| Sparrow Hills | M3 |
| Tchaikovsky Concert Hall | D1 |
| Theater Square | G3 |
| Tolstoy Estate Museum | D7 |
| Tretyakov Gallery | G-H 7 |
| Tsvetnoi Boulevard | H1 |
| White House | A4 |

# GLOSSARY

**alliance:**   Friendship between nations or tribes, based on an agreement to defend one another from enemies

**balalaika:**   Russian instrument with three strings and a long neck, usually played with a pick

**conflagration:**   Major fire

**coup:**   Surprise attack against an existing government

**devastated:**   Destroyed

**essentials:**   Items necessary to daily life

**facet:**   Trait, aspect

**festoon:**   Hang in a decorative fashion

**fresco:**   Painting done on wet plaster

**harangue:**   Long, scolding speech

**jeopardy:**   Danger, risk

**monastery:**   Community of persons who retreat from the world to live a spiritual life

**purge:**   Act of cleansing

**rampant:**   Widespread, uncontrolled

**relentless:**   Unceasing

**revere:**   To feel deep love and respect for

**satire:**   Art or literature that pokes fun at society

**somber:**   Grim, serious

**unassuming:**   Making little attempt to draw attention

## Picture Identifications

**Cover:** St. Basil's Cathedral; a Moscow woman
**Title Page:** Russian girls in national costume
**Pages 4-5:** St. Basill's Cathedral (center) and Red Square
**Pages 8-9:** A Russian woman with a doll dressed in folk costume
**Pages 18-19:** Red Square about 1908
**Pages 32-33:** A performer in the world-famous Moscow Circus
**Pages 44-45:** The Kremlin

# INDEX

*Page numbers in boldface type indicate illustrations*

apartments, 10–11, **10, 11,** 46, 50
Arbat, 50
Arbat Street, 50, 51
Armory Museum, 52, **53**
art 15, 40–43, **43,** 55, 57

Bell Tower of Ivan the Great, **54,** 55, 57
black market, 13
Bolshoi Ballet Company, 34, **35,** 57
Bolshoi Theater, 34, 36, **36,** 57
Bonaparte, Napoleon, 23–24, **23, 24,** 51, 54, 56, 58
Borodino, Battle of, 23–24, **23**
Boulevard Ring, 48
Bulgakov, Mikhail, 38, 50

Cathedral of Christ the Savior, 57, **57**
Chekhov, Anton, 36, 38
children, **1, 6, 15, 49, 55**
Children's Store, 49
Children's Theater, 36, 57
churches, **cover, 4–5,** 10, **41,** 42, **43,** 46, 50–51, **50,** 52, 54, **54,** 55, **55,** 56, **56,** 57, **57**
climate, 16–17, 33, 58
clothes, **1, 6, 16,** 17, **17, 46, 48,** 56
Communism, 10, 13, 14, 26, 27, 38, 40, 42
    fall of, 15, 30, 40, 59
    reforms in, 29, 30
crime, 14

defensive monasteries, 21
Dolgoruki, Yuri, 19, 20, 58
Dzerzhinsky, Felix, 49

Eastern Orthodox Church, 10, 42, 56
economy, 9, 10, 13, **26,** 27, 29, 58
ethnic groups, 10, **11, 15,** 56

Garden Ring, 48
Gorbachev, Mikhail, 29–30, **29, 31, 41,** 59
Gorky, Maxim, 38, **38**
Gorky Park, **16**
Guarenghi, Giacomo, 48
Gulf of Finland, 22

history, 19–31, 57, 58–59
Holy Basil the Fool, 56
housing shortage, 10–11

icons, 42, 43, **43**
inflation, 13
Ivan III, 52
Ivan IV (the Terrible), 21, **21,** 31, 51, 52, 55, 56, 58

Kazan Cathedral, 46, 50–51, **50,** 56
KGB, 31, **31,** 49
Kitay-Gorod, 48
Kolomenskoye, **40,** 46
Kremlin, 5–6, **6–7,** 20, 21, **25,** 28, **44–45,** 51, 52–53, **52, 54,** 55, 58, **59**

Lenin, Vladimir, 14, **14,** 26, **27,** 51
Lenin Hills, 46–47
literature, 33, 36, 38–39, 50
Lubyanka Square, 49
Luzhkov, Yuri, 59
Luzhniki Stadium, 37, **37,** 47, 56

Marx, Karl, 26
Merchants Yard, 15, **15,** 48
Middle Ages, 19
Moscow Arts Theater, 36
Moscow Circus, **32–33,** 34, **34, 35**
Moscow Historical Museum, 51, 56, **56**
Moscow State Symphony, 36
Moscow State University, 47, **47**
Moskva River, 6, 16, 19, 20, 33, **44–45,** 45, 52, 58, **59**
Museum of Applied Folk Art, 56
musicians, 22, 37, **37,** 50

Nicholas II, 26, 27, **27**
Nobel Prize for literature, 38, 59

Olympics, 37, **37,** 56

palaces, 52–53, 54, 56, 57, **57**
parks, 17, 37, 40, 46, **46**
Pasternak, Boris, 38, **38,** 50, 59
*perestroika,* 29, 59
Peter I (the Great), 22, **22,** 51, 58
Politiburo, **28**
population, 10, 58
Pushkin, Alexander, 50, 57
Pushkin Fine Arts Museum, 41, 57

radio, 5, 12
Red Square, **4–5,** 15, **18–19,** 50, 51, 56, **56**
Red Staircase, 54
revolution of 1905, 26, 57, 58
revolution of 1917, 26–27, 38, 41, 57, 58
Rublyov, Andrei, 43

Russia, 5, 6, 10, 19, 20, 23, 28, 30, 38, 58
Russia Hotel, 48, 56

St. Basil's Cathedral, **cover, 4–5, 41, 43,** 51, **55,** 56, **56**
St. George's Hall, 52, 57
St. Petersburg, 22, 58
Savior Tower, 5, 6, 55
shopping, 9–12, 13, 47, 48, 49, 51
Sparrow Hills, 46–47
sports, 17, 33, 37, **37,** 46–47, 56
Stalin, Josef, 28, **28,** 41, 56, 57, 58
Stanislavsky, Konstantin, 36
State Universal Store (GUM), 12, **12,** 13
*Swan Lake,* 34

Tartars, 10, 20, **20,** 52, 58
Tchaikovsky, Peter Ilych, 34
Tchaikovsky Concert Hall, 36
television, 5, 9, 14
Theater Square, 36, 57
Tolstoy, Leo, 39, **39,** 50, 57
transportation, 13, **13,** 15, **15,** 40, 45
Tretyakov Gallery, 42, **42,** 43, 57
tsars, 5, 21, 22, 26, 52, 54, 55, 56
Tsar's Bell, 57
Tsvetnoi Boulevard, 34

Union of Soviet Socialist Republics (USSR), 10, 27, 30, 38

White House, 30, 53
World War II, 28, **28,** 29, **29,** 58

Yeltsin, Boris, 30, **30**

# TO FIND OUT MORE

## BOOKS

Bradley, John. *Russia: Building Democracy.* Austin, Texas: Raintree Steck-Vaughn, 1995.

Burckhardt, Ann L. *The People of Russia and Their Food.* Mankato, Minn.: Capstone Press, 1996.

Butson, Thomas. *Mikhail Gorbachev.* World Leaders Past and Present series. New York: Chelsea House Publishers, 1989.

Clark, James I. *Russia Under the Czars.* Austin, Texas: Raintree Steck-Vaughn, 1990.

Cumming, David. *Russia.* Modern Industrial World series. New York: Thomson Learning, 1994.

Holmes, Burton. *Moscow.* World 100 Years Ago series. New York: Chelsea House Publishers, 1998.

Nadel, Laurie. *The Kremlin Coup.* Brookfield, Conn.: The Millbrook Press, 1992.

Otfinoski, Steven. *Boris Yeltsin and the Rebirth of Russia.* Brookfield, Conn.: The Millbrook Press, 1995.

Torchinskii, Oleg. *Russia.* New York: Marshall Cavendish, 1994.

Vail, John J. *'Peace, Land, Bread!': A History of the Russian Revolution.* New York: Facts on File, 1996.

Venezia, Mike. *Peter Tchaikovsky.* Getting to Know the World's Greatest Composers series. Chicago: Childrens Press, 1994.

Whyte, Harlinah. *Russia.* Festivals of the World series. Milwaukee: Gareth Stevens. 1997.

## ONLINE SITES

**Destination Moscow**
http://www.lonelyplanet.com.au/dest/eur/mos.htm
A Lonely Planet Guide website, this has a wealth of information on Moscow including a map of the city; several pictures; a section on history; facts; the best time to travel to Moscow; a description of the main attractions and museums; Gorky Park; theaters; activities; events; travel information; getting around the city; recommended reading before traveling to Moscow; and more.

**A Journey to Moscow—The Moscow City Tourist Office On-Line**
http://www.moscowcity.com
Includes points of interest with pictures and descriptions: the Kremlin, Red Square, fine arts and museums, theaters, Old Moscow, the Metro (subway system) with its fine art, Lubyanka—the former headquarters of the notorious Soviet police, and Christ the Savior Cathedral; tour suggestions; events throughout the year; useful facts; transportation; and more.

**The Moscow Guide**
http://www.sunsite.cs.msu.su/moscow/
A beautiful site with extensive entries, each with a picture, of the museums of the Moscow Kremlin; the history of Moscow; the Tretyakov Gallery with links to beautiful photographs of five of the paintings in the gallery, each by a different artist; also includes fast facts, reference information about art galleries and museums, churches and cloisters, hotels, restaurants, transportation; and a photo gallery.

## ABOUT THE AUTHOR

Deborah Kent grew up in Little Falls, New Jersey, and received a B.A. in English from Oberlin College. She earned a master's degree from Smith College School for Social Work. After working for four years at the University Settlement House in New York City, she moved to San Miguel de Allende in central Mexico. There she wrote her first young-adult novel, *Belonging.* Ms. Kent is the author of many titles in the Children's Press Cities of the World series. She lives in Chicago with her husband, author R. Conrad Stein, and their daughter Janna.